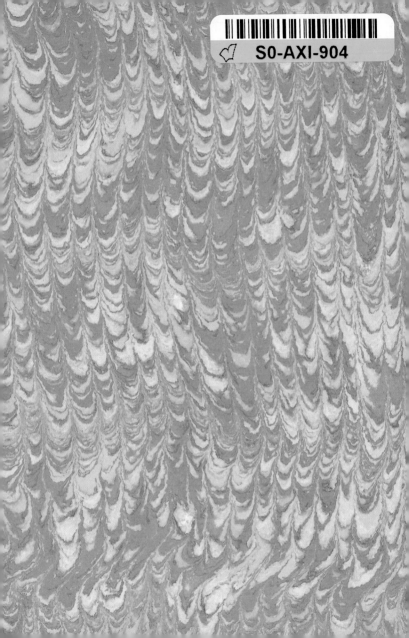

This copy of

MORE PRECIOUS THAN GOLD

comes to

Connie Ann

July 2015

with love from

Anna, a long-time friend!

MORE PRECIOUS THAN GOLD

Copyright © 1996 by Eagle

Published by Crossway Books
a division of Good News Publishers
1300 Crescent Street
Wheaton, Illinois 60187

First British edition published by Eagle, 1996

First U.S. edition published by Crossway Books, 1998

First U.S. printing, 1998

Printed in Singapore

Scripture quotations are taken from the following versions: NIV, New
International Version; JER, Jerusalem Bible; RSV, Revised Standard Version;
GNB, Good News Bible.

The "NIV" and "New International Version" trademarks are registered in the
United States Patent and Trademark Office by International Bible Society. Use of
either trademark requires the permission of International Bible Society.

LIBRARY OF CONGRESS CATALOGING-IN-PUBLICATION DATA
More precious than gold : Psalms of praise and hope. — 1st U.S. ed.
    p.   cm.
  I. Crossway Books.   II. Bible. O.T. Psalms. Selections. 1998.
BSI423.M67 1998   223'.2052—dc21   97-38478
ISBN 0-89107-988-2

08	07	06	05	04	03	02	01	00	99	98
15	14	13	12	11	10	9	8	7	6	5	4	3	2	1

MORE PRECIOUS THAN GOLD

Psalms of Praise and Hope

CROSSWAY BOOKS

IN YOU, O LORD

In you, O LORD, I have taken refuge; let me never be put to shame; deliver me in your righteousness. Turn your ear to me, come quickly to my rescue; be my rock of refuge, a strong fortress to save me. Since you are my rock and my fortress, for the sake of your name lead and guide me.

Be merciful to me, O LORD, for I am in distress; my eyes grow weak with sorrow, my soul and my body with grief.

But I trust in you, O LORD; I say, "You are my God." My times are in your hands. . . .

Praise be to the LORD, for he showed his wonderful love to me. . . . In my alarm I said, "I am cut off from your sight!" Yet you heard my cry for mercy when I called to you for help.

PSALM 31:1-3, 9, 14-15, 21-22 NIV

Llandudno Junction, North Wales, Thomas Baker

I WAITED PATIENTLY

❧

I waited patiently for the LORD; he turned to me and heard my cry. He lifted me out of the slimy pit, out of the mud and mire; he set my feet on a rock and gave me a firm place to stand. He put a new song in my mouth, a hymn of praise to our God. Many will see and fear and put their trust in the LORD.

Blessed is the man who makes the LORD his trust, who does not look to the proud, to those who turn aside to false gods. Many, O LORD my God, are the wonders you have done. The things you planned for us no one can recount to you; were I to speak and tell of them, they would be too many to declare.

PSALM 40:1-5 NIV

A Winding Gorge, 1919, Harold Sutton Palmer

I WILL EXALT YOU, O LORD

❧

I will exalt you, O LORD, . . . O LORD my God, I called to you for help and you healed me. O LORD, you brought me up from the grave; you spared me from going down into the pit. Sing to the LORD, you saints of his; praise his holy name. For his anger lasts only a moment, but his favor lasts a lifetime; weeping may remain for a night, but rejoicing comes in the morning. When I felt secure, I said, "I shall never be shaken." O LORD, when you favored me, you made my mountain stand firm; but when you hid your face, I was dismayed.

To you, O LORD, I called; to the LORD I cried for mercy: . . . You turned my wailing into dancing; you removed my sackcloth and clothed me with joy, that my heart may sing to you and not be silent. O LORD my God, I will give you thanks forever.

PSALM 30:1-8, 11-12 NIV

The Evening Glow, Perth, Alfred de Breanski

WE BOAST OF THE NAME
OF THE LORD

The LORD answer you in the day of trouble! The name of the God of Jacob protect you! May he send you help from the sanctuary, and give you support from Zion! May he remember all your offerings, and regard with favor your burnt sacrifices!

May he grant you your heart's desire, and fulfill all your plans! May we shout for joy over your victory, and in the name of our God set up our banners! May the LORD fulfill all your petitions! . . .

Some boast of chariots, and some of horses; but we boast of the name of the LORD our God. They will collapse and fall; but we shall rise and stand upright.

PSALM 20:1-5, 7-8 RSV

Happy Days!, Theodore-Louis Deyrolle

GOD IS OUR REFUGE

❧

God is our refuge and strength, a very present help in trouble. Therefore we will not fear though the earth should change, though the mountains shake in the heart of the sea; though its water roar and foam, though the mountains tremble with its tumult.

There is a river whose streams make glad the city of God, the habitation of the Most High. God is in the midst of her, she shall not be moved; God will help her right early. The nations rage, the kingdoms totter; he utters his voice, the earth melts. The LORD of hosts is with us; the God of Jacob is our refuge. . . .

"Be still, and know that I am God. I am exalted among the nations, I am exalted in the earth!"

PSALM 46:1-7, 10 RSV

A Stormy Landscape, Robert Gallon

SHOUT FOR JOY TO THE LORD

Shout for joy to the LORD, all the earth.
Worship the LORD with gladness;
come before him with joyful songs.
Know that the LORD is God.
It is he who made us, and we are his;
we are his people, the sheep of his pasture.

Enter his gates with thanksgiving
and his courts with praise;
give thanks to him and praise his name.
For the LORD is good and his love endures forever;
his faithfulness continues through all generations.

PSALM 100 NIV

Amberly Castle, 1897, Alfred East

HOW GOOD, HOW DELIGHTFUL

❧

How good, how delightful it is
for all to live together like brothers:

fine as oil on the head,
running down the beard,
running down Aaron's beard
to the collar of his robes;

copious as a Hermon dew
falling on the heights of Zion
where Yahweh confers his blessing,
everlasting life.

PSALM 133 JER

———————————

A View of Chamonix and Mont Blanc, Joseph Jansen

The Law of the Lord

The law of the LORD is perfect, reviving the soul. The statutes of the LORD are trustworthy, making wise the simple. The precepts of the LORD are right, giving joy to the heart. The commands of the LORD are radiant, giving light to the eyes. The fear of the LORD is pure, enduring forever. The ordinances of the LORD are sure and altogether righteous. They are more precious than gold, than much pure gold; they are sweeter than honey, than honey from the comb. By them is your servant warned; in keeping them there is great reward. . . .

May the words of my mouth and the meditation of my heart be pleasing in your sight, O LORD, my Rock and my Redeemer.

PSALM 19:7-11, 14 NIV

Far from the Madding Crowd, William Affleck

UNLESS THE LORD BUILDS
THE HOUSE

❧

Unless the Lord builds the house,

its builders labor in vain.

Unless the Lord watches over the city,

the watchmen stand guard in vain. . . .

Sons are a heritage from the Lord,

children a reward from him.

Like arrows in the hands of a warrior

are sons born in one's youth.

PSALM 127:1, 3-4 NIV

Picking Posies, William Kay Blacklock

LORD, THOU HAST SEARCHED ME AND KNOWN ME

O LORD, thou hast searched me and known me! Thou knowest when I sit down and when I rise up; thou discernest my thoughts from afar. Thou searchest out my path and my lying down, and art acquainted with all my ways. . . .

For thou didst form my inward parts, thou didst knit me together in my mother's womb. . . .

How precious to me are thy thoughts, O God! How vast is the sum of them! If I would count them, they are more than the sand. When I awake, I am still with thee. . . .

Search me, O God, and know my heart! Try me and know my thoughts! And see if there be any wicked way in me, and lead me in the way everlasting!

PSALM 139:1-3, 13, 17-18, 23-24 RSV

Lazy Days, William Marshall Brown

SING A NEW SONG

❧

Sing a new song to the LORD! Sing to the LORD, all the world! Sing to the LORD, and praise him! Proclaim every day the good news that he has saved us. Proclaim his glory to the nations, his mighty deeds to all peoples.

The LORD is great and is to be highly praised; . . . Glory and majesty surround him; power and beauty fill his Temple. . . .

Say to all the nations, "The LORD is king! The earth is set firmly in place and cannot be moved; he will judge the peoples with justice." Be glad, earth, and sky! Roar, sea, and every creature in you; be glad, fields, and everything in you! The trees in the woods will shout for joy when the LORD comes to rule the earth. He will rule the peoples of the world with justice and fairness.

PSALM 96:1-4, 6, 10-13 GNB

Richmond, Yorkshire, Edmund John Niemann

PRAISE THE LORD, O MY SOUL

Praise the LORD, O my soul. O LORD my God, you are very great; you are clothed with splendor and majesty. . . . He makes springs pour water into the ravines; it flows between the mountains. They give water to all the beasts of the field; the wild donkeys quench their thirst. The birds of the air nest by the waters; they sing among the branches. . . .

The trees of the LORD are well watered, the cedars of Lebanon that he planted. There the birds make their nest; the stork has its home in the pine trees. The high mountains belong to the wild goats; the crags are a refuge for the coneys. . . .

How many are your works, O LORD! In wisdom you made them all; the earth is full of your creatures. There is the sea, vast and spacious, teeming with creatures beyond number—living things both large and small. . . .

May the glory of the LORD endure forever; may the LORD rejoice in his works.

PSALM 104:1, 10-12, 16-18, 24-25, 31 NIV

Birches of the Dee, Alfred de Breanski

WHO MAY DWELL IN YOUR SANCTUARY?

LORD, who may dwell in your sanctuary?
Who may live on your holy hill?

He whose walk is blameless
and who does what is righteous,
who speaks the truth from his heart
and has no slander on his tongue,
who does his neighbor no wrong
and casts no slur on his fellowman,
who despises a vile man
but honors those who fear the LORD,
who keeps his oath even when it hurts,
who lends his money without usury
and does not accept a bribe against the innocent.

He who does these things will never be shaken.

PSALM 15 NIV

In the Orchard, Valentine Davis

PRAISE GOD IN HIS SANCTUARY

Praise the Lord.

Praise God in his sanctuary;
praise him in his mighty heavens.
Praise him for his acts of power;
praise him for his surpassing greatness.
Praise him with the sounding of the trumpet,
praise him with the harp and lyre,
praise him with tambourine and dancing,
praise him with the strings and flute,
praise him with the clash of cymbals,
praise him with resounding cymbals.

Let everything that has breath praise the Lord.

Praise the Lord.

PSALM 150 NIV

Still Life, and Ever and Anon the Wind, Sweet Scented Wind
John Edward Newton

PHOTOGRAPHIC CREDITS

Crossway Books is grateful to the copyright holders listed below, and to The Fine Art Photographic Library in particular for their kind permission to reproduce the paintings selected to complement the text.

COVER   *Lazy Days*, by William Marshall Brown, 1863-1936, Burlington Paintings, London.

1.   *Llandudno Junction, North Wales*, by Thomas Baker, 1809-1869, St Peter's Fine Art, Chester.

2.   *A Winding Gorge, 1919*, by Harold Sutton Palmer, 1854-1933.

3.   *The Evening Glow*, by Alfred de Breanski, 1852-1928, Private Collection.

4.   *Happy Days!*, by Theodore-Louis Deyrolle, ?-1923, Burlington Gallery, London.

5.   *A Stormy Landscape*, by Robert Gallon, 1845-1925.

6.   *Amberly Castle, 1897*, by Alfred East, 1849-1913, Polak Gallery, London.

7.   *A View of Chamonix and Mont Blanc*, by Joseph Jansen, 1829-1905, Colin Stodgell Gallery.

8.   *Far from the Madding Crowd*, by William Affleck, 1868-1943, Haynes Fine Art.

9.   *Picking Posies*, by William Kay Blacklock, 1872-1924, Haynes Fine Art.

10.   *Lazy Days*, by William Marshall Brown, 1863-1936, Burlington Paintings, London.

11.   *Richmond, Yorkshire*, by Edmund John Niemann, 1813-1876, Burlington Paintings, London.

12.   *Birches of the Dee*, by Alfred de Breanski, 1852-1928, Burlington Paintings, London.

13.   *In the Orchard*, by Valentine Davis, 1854-1930, Haynes Fine Art, Broadway.

14.   *Still Life, and Ever and Anon the Wind, Sweet Scented Wind*, by John Edward Newton, 1835-1891.